I Can Read!

LUCY MAUD MONTGOMERY:
CREATOR OF *ANNE OF GREEN GABLES*

by Sarah Howden
pictures by Nick Craine

Collins

Maud is playing outside.

She doesn't have any playmates,

so she is talking to the trees.

"Your name is Charlie,"
Maud tells an oak.
"And you are Eliza,"
she tells a maple.

"You are about to go on a
great adventure," says Maud.
Maud loves telling stories.
She has a big imagination.

Maud lives on Prince Edward Island
with her grandparents.

Her full name is Lucy Maud.

But she prefers Maud.

Maud has no brothers or sisters.
But she has imaginary friends to
play with if she's lonely.

They live behind the glass of

the bookcase door.

She calls their home the fairy room.

"Hi, Katie and Lucy," Maud says.
Her imaginary friends smile
back at her.

Maud has a lot of books.

She loves to read and write.

"I wrote a new story!"

Maud tells her grandma.

"I'll read it to you."

"You have a keen imagination,"
Maud's grandma says.
"I want to be an author,"
Maud tells her.

13

When Maud grows up,
she has different jobs.
She is a teacher and
a newspaper reporter.

Maud also takes care of her grandma.

But she never stops writing.

One day Maud thinks up a
very special story.
"I will write about a girl
like me," she says to herself.

"I will call her Anne."

"Anne will be smart

and silly and brave,"

Maud says.

"Anne will love nature
and books," Maud says.
"And she'll have a temper,
with fiery red hair to match."

Maud calls her story
Anne of Green Gables.
She is proud of her work.

Maud sends her story

to publishers.

Publishers make books.

But the publishers send it back.

"No, thank you," they say.

"We don't like your story."

Maud is sad.

She puts her story away in a box.

Then one day Maud is cleaning.

She finds the story in the box.

She decides to try again.

Maud sends the story out.
And this time a good letter
comes back.

This publisher loves the story.

"Oh my!" Maud says.

She jumps up and down.

Anne of Green Gables is printed.

The book is sold in stores.

Everyone loves it.

It isn't just popular in Canada.

It's popular all over the world!

"Could you write another book?"
her publisher asks.

"I'd love to!" Maud says.

29

Maud writes more books about Anne.

She writes other books too.

Her readers know her as

L.M. Montgomery.

Maud is happy.

Her dream has come true.

She is finally a famous author.

And best of all, Maud is
doing what she loves.
She is telling stories.

Dear Parent:
Your child's love of reading starts here!

Every child learns to read in a different way and at his or her own speed. Some go back and forth between reading levels and read favourite books again and again. Others read through each level in order. You can help your young reader improve and become more confident by encouraging his or her own interests and abilities. From books your child reads with you to the first books he or she reads alone, there are I Can Read Books for every stage of reading:

SHARED READING
Basic language, word repetition, and whimsical illustrations, ideal for sharing with your emergent reader

BEGINNING READING
Short sentences, familiar words, and simple concepts for children eager to read on their own

READING WITH HELP
Engaging stories, longer sentences, and language play for developing readers

READING ALONE
Complex plots, challenging vocabulary, and high-interest topics for the independent reader

I Can Read Books have introduced children to the joy of reading since 1957. Featuring award-winning authors and illustrators and a fabulous cast of beloved characters, I Can Read Books set the standard for beginning readers.

A lifetime of discovery begins with the magical words "I Can Read!"

Visit www.icanread.ca for information
on enriching your child's reading experience.

I Can Read Book® is a trademark of HarperCollins Publishers

Lucy Maud Montgomery: Creator of Anne of Green Gables
Text copyright © 2019 by HarperCollins Publishers Ltd.
Pictures © 2019 by Nick Craine.
All rights reserved. Published by Collins, an imprint of HarperCollins Publishers Ltd.

HarperCollins books may be purchased for educational, business, or sales promotional use through our Special Markets Department.

HarperCollins Publishers Ltd
Bay Adelaide Centre, East Tower
22 Adelaide Street West, 41st Floor
Toronto, Ontario, Canada
M5H 4E3

www.harpercollins.ca

Library and Archives Canada Cataloguing in Publication information is available upon request.

www.icanread.ca

ISBN 978-1-4434-5984-6

WZL 1 2 3 4 5 6 7 8 9 10